THE RAG TREE SPEAKS

THE RAG TREE SPEAKS

Emma McKervey

Doire Press

First published in 2017

Doire Press
Aille, Inverin
Co. Galway
www.doirepress.com

Layout & design: Lisa Frank
Cover art: Philip Mussen
Author photo: Philip Mussen

Printed by Clódóirí CL
Casla, Co. na Gaillimhe

ISBN 978-1-907682-55-1

We gratefully acknowledge the support and assistance of The Arts Council of Northern Ireland.

LOTTERY FUNDED

CONTENTS

To my mother, Jeannette McKervey

An Sciathán

It can be considered odd that the Irish language
has no word for hand or foot; these appendages,
as we see them, are of the linguistic flow of arm and leg
and the words themselves seem supple and warm,
suggestive of the dexterity of the limbs as a whole;
undisjointed, unsegmented and all to a singular purpose.
In Ulster Irish there is a different word for arm (and hand)
which translates most easily as 'wing'.
This may explain the hunch in my shoulders in the North,
the roil of blade and faint domino click of vertebrae
when trying to rotate the ball in its socket.
The feathers grow inwards, abstruse quills prickle
beneath the skin so when we talk and my arms wave
to ballast my point, I cannot suddenly rise up —
fly away.

Ernest Wilson Goes to China

There had been despair when at last he'd reached
the site of the tree and discovered instead a new home
constructed of well-seasoned planks of timber
which his elderly scribbled map had not allowed for.

Behind him lay Yunan, disease, bandits, shipwreck
and the incomprehensible language so abrupt he couldn't hear
when speech turned to laughter, then back to speech.
He suspected laughter most of the time.

His specimen case bulged with many things
but it was only as he finally swung into the branches
with arboreal ease in a secret copse at the brink of a cliff
(last autumn's segments of fruit already scooped and bagged),

that he could see the bracts as white doves falling
until in the river they sailed; paper lanterns lit from within.
From the crook of the tree his own diamond body gleamed.

The Statues

The wedge of granite dark Cathedral is propped on its perch
by a myriad of flying buttresses at the crest of the hill.

It is overcast this day and the way to the door is dark,
the statues along the avenue brood in religious gloom,

lost in contemplation of cobbles polished by penitents' feet,
until cloud break allows the invisible to come to light —

the crown on the lion's mane, a sceptre in bishop's hand,
the hilt of a king's sword, a haloed head of a nameless saint —

all illuminated in sudden gold, and, from Prague, I long for home;
the phosphorescent wake of my Uncle's fishing boat

as it leaves the Lough at dusk, and, when I turn,
Ailsa Craig emerging, like Mount Fuji, through the mists.

Ex-Lovers' Car Boot Sale

Beautiful feathered wings are common here
propped against bumpers, faded and perhaps bedraggled,
with missing quills and popped fastenings.
Dusty jewels cascade from tatty boxes stacked on tables
normally used for camping trips and picnics,
which are also for sale, alongside the tartan blankets.

One woman has bottled the sheen of the morning sun,
refracted off her hair spread across Egyptian cotton pillows.
It's labelled, dated, and available for a knock-down price.
She slumps on the tail light, one foot rests on a low stool,
queued in a row of pedestals of varying heights.

We trudge the field this Sunday morning, picking over
recycled treasure troves; golden casts of breasts
and haunches in sensuous curve — tarnished and chipped,
stardust from love dazed eyes which is now in Tupperware
and rustles with the scratch of dried herbs when shaken.

One case is accidentally knocked from its perch,
laughter from a shared joke causes stall holders
and customers to glance up momentarily
before it is scraped back into its holdings, resealed,
and sold for half the asking value, intimacy lost.

The food is good though, elaborate fried breakfasts,
strawberries and cream, oysters and French cheeses —
it's why we come here, and for the secrets;
what is tucked away in glove compartments
or under seats, hoarded stores of scraps

which they will not show until prompted,
reluctant to be handed over for perusal —
the sense of warm breath on the spine,
the final closing of a door,
unwilling to sell at any cost.

Buenos Aires

He had grown up in Buenos Aires
in the brothel of his grandfather,
where the woman pinched his cheeks
and men tossed coins and sweets
across the floor for him to gather.

Real men, he had thought, real men
who swaggered through doorways
opened beer bottles with a flick of a thumb
and laughed heartily at their own jokes.

All day and night the household groaned;
a ship in a storm, rigging twisted
and whistling in the wind's embrace,
thrumming between tension and release,
punctured with high pitched wails.

The thighs of the women
seemed to straddle his grandfather's house
hold it steady, fix it firm to the earth
but he rarely thinks of it now,

except sometimes on a train journey
from where he lives now, far to the East
when the rain peppers the windows
and the pretty girls shriek with laugher,
their water bottles warming on their lips.

Superstition

I never actually thought I was knocking
the devil off my shoulder
with a pinch of spilled salt,
but the motion
made me feel I belonged somehow,
my small gesture tying me to
the small gestures of many years
my grandmothers may have made.
Maybe all that salt we've tossed
has been stacking up,
rebuilding a scattered saline pillar
and some day if my daughter dares look behind
she will see it once again transformed
into a complete woman.

The Rag Tree Speaks

Cerebus uses me to urinate against;
he releases his stinking stream of piss, one head
watching its trickling through the crackles of my bark,
the other intent on whether the chrome yellow trail
can reach the river's edge where the ferryman waits.
He sniffs my sides, lingering to the North where the lichen
and moss grow thickest to assert none other has used me
as their staging post, then, satisfied, bounds back to the shore.
It is a slight revenge in this Underworld,
as they cannot dig out my roots,
I'm embedded and protected by too many charms,
my reflection bonded too strongly in the sunlit side
where my passing would be noticed —
the entrance would be dug out from sodden trough,
the dry heave of stump overturned —
then where would they be, exposed to the light?
They have ways around it though;
my brother was felled in Clonenagh
they reckoned he'd died (or that was implied),
from all the coins hammered into his boughs
down here avoiding the ferryman's fee.
The newly dead had laughed before,
merry in his shade, camped on the banks
with the toll untaken, and here across the Styx
my dead were glad too, beneath their streamered hopes —
until one day he was gone and Charon
stood counting the glistening heaps of gold,
his mutt snapping and nosing them onto the boat.
On my shore they cling to the flash and flicker
of all they've tied fast to help them recall.
I hold their rags as long as I can;
when the rags fall, rotten with time,
they need to forget, as what's left becomes unbearable —
they turn from me, wander to the distant shore

and drink deep from the mercury sludge
of the Lethe River's flow.

Aquatic Ape Theory

The water in my house moves slow,
the bath takes an age to drain,
the cistern an hour to fill,
and each tap drizzles lacklustre
when coffee grains need sweeping away.

I wonder what secret creatures
lurk in the plumbing of my home
drinking deep of the clean water's flow
and misdirecting the suds with cunning
slight of hand.

Imagine the landscape Noah beheld
in the Flood's ebbing tide;
the bloated remains of the unsaved
half-feasted on by those fish whose gills
may not have been an oversight
but were allowed to remain with a managerial eye
on the need for a thorough clean-up.

Perhaps some fast evolving ape
embraced the aquatic to survive
with inter-toe webbing
and prodigious lungs

who continued to evolve with Time
until becoming the clandestine miniature
of themselves who live in my pipes,
who think I believe myself made in His image
and seek a quiet revenge.

Lenticulate

Lenticulae is Latin for freckles
my arms are lenticulated
as are my nose and forehead
and there are lenticular strata
scattered about the horseshoe
pause in my collarbone.
I imagine your fingertips there
studying the pattern and joining the dots,
articulating the ancient constellations
rendered on my skin.
You are alchemist and astrographer —
you read the Jovian calligraphy
of my lenticulae and understand
I am the moon Europa and
you are Galilei.
You've named me for a lover of Zeus
regardless my frozen oceans,
you wait for my elliptical orbit
to complete day after day,
can trace the lines of chaos
when they break through.
You watch and wait and I feel beautiful
framed in the lens of your gaze.
Lenticulae is Latin for freckles.
My body is the chart of your touch.

Chopping Wood

There is a rhythmic sound escaped from childhood book
jarring in the magnolia vacuum of suburbia.
The Woodcutter, sweaty browed and shirtless,
systematically swings his axe, fracturing the logs
with powerful golden arcs. Beyond the boundary
of backyard fence the Wildwoods encroach.

I view him from my window, the bed partially stripped,
feather duvet hanging in gibbous eclipse,
whilst, standing disguised in the curtain's shade,
I hope to remain unseen; I watch the wolves
and lost children drawing close in the trees, waiting
as the balance shifts from hewn to cloven with every blow.

With each severed block stacked the forest recedes
the creatures and the changelings are gone.
At night his shadow plays on drawn blinds
projected by the twitching glow of television screen.

Bear

The skin cools where exhalation skims,
where non-retractable claws take their heavy rest.
There is wonder at the puckering of flesh,
indented by such casual weight beneath lethargic barb.
How long to let them lay there without check;
if the solid steady force of forgetting
punctures eventually the skin,
the sleek accidental slide of razor tip into epidermis
pillows with sudden beaded cadmium of blood,
would this stare still be transfixed at the spilling
of humour collecting in puddles of escape —
the small chill of dying kisses stained sticky red
by fading pulse? A trail of lovers' names
gathers on the tongue each waiting
for their summons — let them wait in silence —
let the names remain uncalled,
watch the press of those sleeping paws,
that mouth, that warm and somnolent breath
take ease against your chest.

Pale Blue Fragments

The full span of seasons passed
but when Spring came round again
you did not return.

And though I walked the land,
searched the hedgerows and lanes,
scrambled through briar patches

and peered across fields which were murky
with the mud of Winter's sodden turf
you did not return.

I thought maybe you would come at night
carried by owl with gormlessly hanging beak
cadging a supper of flies

but when I checked the morning's window ledge
hoping for a sulky perch
you had not returned.

The furze bushes still bloomed though
and the crocus heads still bowed
under their own ecstatic show.

I still brought home the pale blue fragments
of hatched eggs and put out scraps for the birds.
You did not return.

Questioning the Rain

Its hows, and wherefores; and its relentless willingness to embrace,

discard and pour; its sound the rinsing hiss and condensed crackle-like-tinfoil as it strikes impediments on its journey. Its imperative and entitlement is consuming and it spreads as a membrane on the soil, street, tiles and raised umbrellas, binding each to the other in huddled defence.

It is endless, and pauses between showers merely just that; a pause between drips and droplets, merely a lengthier passage of time before the space is filled once more with the dispersal of water, the previous drop is followed once again by another, a viscous reclamation and control

regardless if the earth is cracked and resistant or damply, spongily seeping; imbibed, imbued, impregnated and sodden, the velocity and circumference of each point of falling water dictates its own weeping mesh to bind the sky to the world.

Scalph, or Maybe Love

The idea of poking with tweezers at the small scalph
on my ring finger seemed undignified somehow,
a heavy handed and violent act against such a tiny fragment
of what had once been a living thing,
barely noticeable in the digit's pad not far beneath the tip.
The body will naturally know how to push out
such a minuscule invader, benignly dealing with Nature's
mild transgression which barely impedes upon my day
was my reasoning, and let it be, pleased
when it snagged on the fine azure blue of a silk scarf
as this meant the scalph was gradually
being ejected from its rest.
I had not understood the tenacity
of the willow when it came to growth
(for it was from the willow this jagged shard had come),
so it took some days before the lime verdancy
of the tiny sprout was seen, the fine shoot twirling
its fastidious way through the loops
of my finger's whirling print.
My ring finger quickly became weighted
with the burgeoning bough
fecund and catkin-laden in the season's balmy air.
So I learned to hold my unfurling hand aloft,
accept the skin's slow toughening to bark,
welcome the bees and caterpillars
who took rest beneath my leaves
and not to grieve when those leaves
turned golden brown and fell.
I learned to hold the naked spindles dear
when made brittle in the Winter's frost,
to wait for the sap in Spring to rise, and, smiling,
welcome the greening spread
from finger pad to each straining twig's
reddening buds once more.

The Pithos Jar

It was no mistake, the trickster god
delivering speech to Pandora,
the Hermetic message service unleashed.
She may not even have needed
to open the box really
once a voice was found,
as language is a complex thing.
Indeed it is through a mistranslation
that the pithos jar became a box
to contain all that Pandora would release,
claiming the innocence of curiosity in her defence.
Even what was left is questionable in translation —
Hope should have been Expectation,
which is a little less poetic,
and carries a sense of entitlement,
despite the chaos which was set free.
It was Diogenes of Sinope
who made a pithos his home,
so perhaps satisfaction
can be taken from the knowledge
it was the original Cynic who slept
at the bottom of that jar,
curled around the only thing left to us —
Expectation (or sometimes Hope),
the flame of which lit the lamp
he carried in the daylight
in search of an honest man.

Cedar Wood

It is odd that the cedar wood is cut,
carved, and sanded into acorns of around 3 cm
as the acorn is the fruit of the oak tree.
It does make an underwear drawer
emit a pleasant scent
whilst rummaging in the early morning
in the throes of pre-work tension.
The cedar acorns huddle in the gloom
of lace and stretched elastic, and sometimes
when a moment of peace is required
one can be removed from its cloistered sleep
and rolled dreamily between the palms
to warm the grain and loosen the sap
in silent stasis within before continuing
the hunt for matching socks.
Solomon commanded 80,000 men to cut down
the cedar trees of Lebanon for him.
Then the whole nation must have been permeated
with the fresh scent in the air against the crash
of falling trees, sinuses alternatively sawdust clogged
and then cleansed with the fragrant breeze
as the hills were denuded of wood.
With these razed trees he wished to build a palace
in which he could find peace and rolled
in the space between the palms of those boughs
wisdom sought might possibly have been found.
Such knowledge is good to hold on to
when drawers refuse to shut against
the tendrils of stockings;
that for a king 80,000 men
and several forests of timber
is needed to find clarity of thought
when three small acorns can so often be enough.

Epistemological Inadequacies

We stood by the sink waiting for the kettle to boil.
I was relieved he had his back to the teabag's
spreading stain leaving a neglected rust on the metal rim.
The conversation still remains unclear in my mind though,
oscillating as it did between the minutiae of school pick-ups
and the nature of love and its epistemological inadequacies.
He appeared not to notice my straying gaze
as we idled by the sinking grains in the coffee pot.
It can only be considered unfortunate that behind him —
a half-metre back, hovering to the upper right of his ear,
a fly had become trapped in sticky web
which straddled the window frame and blind,
caught in its late season adventures
and now was being tightly bound.
He was unaware my attention had moved,
snared by the bluebottle's demise
as instinctively and methodically the spider busied itself
with the minutiae of its life and survival —
an enabler's role in a profound and symbolic death.

Spinsters

In this week by the lake tiny spiders have netted my skin.
At first I picked them off and settled them carefully
on some invisible current of air to ply their spindle elsewhere.
But now I let them roam at will, leaving their fine tracery
to bind my limbs and stream in the ripples of my wake;
tresses of a beached mermaid spinning beyond the tide line
and reaching along the shore.

The breeze carries these silken threads, spreads
my *sfumato* image across the forest;
the curve of bicep hangs loose from a young larch,
my shoulder blade caught in the crook of a pine,
and my nape swung free out over the water —
suspended now, taut, between the reeds.

Rathlin Island

There was a brief glimpse, and then,
with shifting the line of sight
to accommodate the patch of gorse,
both hares, boxing, could be viewed.
There was compact power in the haunches of each,
upright, above the sheep-nibbled grass —
beneath the sunlight the blonde coats shimmered.
Through the breath-grimed window
at the back of the bus, somewhere between
one jolt and another on that ageing lane
a single hare turned, found my gaze,
fixed it with his Nordic stare.
This is the amulet I keep now about my neck,
invisible against my breastbone.
This is my talisman: the hare's regard,
the unfractured sky, the swaying sea,
and the tiny speedwell scattered
through the velvet turf.

Belief in Glass

Glass is not a liquid, despite the popular belief
in which those medieval cathedral windows
are pouring ever downwards with agonising slowness,
the belief that one day those windows
will drip across the leading and down the hewn walls,
imperceptibly at first, then increasing speed
with the rising joy of escape, replacing the murals
which had covered the walls long ago,
vanishing with the years' unfolding.

The glass would trickle a pathway,
the top of each window thinning until a bloom
of sunlight, unfiltered, can ease its way through,
illuminating the intimate choreography
of incense and cobweb.
The Stations of the Cross will blend,
figures melding and drifting,
loosening crucifixes and soldiers,
the pious and the thieves
until the oxides of gold, silver, copper and manganese
bleed into one another's embrace.

But the windows are fixed firm from Bull's Eye of Pontil Rod;
the rippling a result of the centrifugal force
which flattened out the bubble of glass as it was spun
and will always shatter when something hard is flung,
as glass is not liquid, despite the popular belief.

Hera and Persephone

My eyes stare out from the fanning peacock's tail;
she is wilfully unaware of the silver thread
which binds us by blood, or whichever familial bonds
the Hellenic gods possess to recognise their tribe.

I preside over the marital bed of her winter hibernation
fallow, with her legs spread wide, waiting for Spring.
She has forgotten the pomegranate was held in my hand
long before she spat its seeds to the earth claimed as her own

and now she has ordinance in her chthonic kingdom,
my peacocks wailing about her feet, my fruit split, scattered,
my watching her, my niece, as she blithely dances
along the terminus between the dark and the light.

Needles of Bone

She wonders if this is productive enough
when what she wanted was nothing
except maybe to learn how the men shoot
snot from one nostril, pinning the other shut.
It seemed unfair when all she had was her hem.
In the damp corner of a field, seeking warmth
from the heaped hay, she found the bones of a bird,
more substantial than if it had been the stripped bones
of a stolen fledgling the magpies had taken
to ease the dark hunger in themselves.
The larger bones would make a fine needle
she could not help but think, but as she worked
the gentle corpse it was not needles or pins she made,
but a chain, each eye she pierced she found herself
sliding the next bone through, it formed a line
to cut across the silage. She left it there when she rose,
intending to return home.

Advice to a Young Climber

If one rocks onto the balls of one's feet,
and hunkers down low, it is possible to reduce
the full electrical shock of a lightning strike.
It is, however, entirely dependent on the force
of that strike and the strength of one's heart to survive.
Certain knowledge to read the signs of the hills
is needed by any wary climber,
who is mindful of their health, to spot the threat of a storm:
the banking of cumulonimbus above the crest
should indicate it is time to return,
to take the downward path,
to avoid the trees, the caves, the mines,
as those boughs and thresholds can shatter,
splintering to three million pieces about one's head.
So, keep the mass of mountain above oneself,
watch the skies and the rise of the peaks
and head home, head home, head home

Clearances

The rookery had cleared, what had been one
of the largest colonies recorded in Europe
was now abandoned. Only sheep grazed
about the girth of the horse chestnuts
where the trunks entered the earth,
delicate hooves crunching on the litter
of untended nests as gradually the snapped sticks fell.
All the scoops of bark and trammelled twigs
which had been chosen, lifted,
fitted carefully into the chaotic neighbourhood
of so many foragers — disintegrating.
The tricksters who could break shells
open on the rocks to feast on the soft insides,
who artificed hooks of wire with which to fish
small seeds and worms from awkward spots
have moved on — within the stacked
and cramped estate the bony beaks no longer protrude.
It is not silent with the absence of their flattened, maddening caw;
the sheep bleat, the martins and swallows make their incessant chatter,
but the sky is undarkened by their wing,
the Autumn gales are unridden.

Comet

Coasting the reel of golden thread to the realm of the dead,
suspended in air from that line of faith came the inheritors of the stars;

but the windlassed fall remained unfixed,
the dark flight of meandering over-shot orbs

strobed in cosmic dust: the yellow of iron,
the violet of calcium and the splattered cadmium red

of nitrogen and oxygen — each pin-pointed
mote of this non-ephemeral rainbow —

remained, despite disintegration,
significantly larger than an atom.

Nearing Earth these objects unspooled,
targeted in trajectory and curve of light,

the thread unguided and lost, leaving the glistering
frayed remnants to be ground into the weary clay.

The Ghost of a Bee

The corpses of bees can be easily confused
with the tiny dropped cones of the alder tree
as the gold diminishes in death, and the husk,
which is what remains after the even tinier mites
have had their fill, ossifies to indeterminate brown.
It is no matter, this brittle hollow;
the ghost of a bee holds out its acorn cup
and receives the aureate honey drip from the living hive,
small offerings to memory made by the hum of bees
a soft thanks sung beneath the susurration of work.

Unravelling

The small hole in the corner of the coat's deep pocket
was worked at until a space wide enough for a thumb's diameter
was created. And then, in the lining, a loose thread was tugged
to cause a little unravelling along the seam,
not really noticeable to an eye which may be uninterested.
This was after the dried beans, which had been forgotten
in the pocket from the previous season,
had been discovered, dormant in the cool, dry dark.

By walking at a certain pace those brown beans
could now accidentally fall through the hole
which was the approximate width of a thumb
and from there perhaps tumble where the seam
was unravelled at the hem and out of the coat entirely.

There may be at this time, in the wake of the unmended
and perambulating coat, beanstalks rising from the pavement
cracks and silty gutters, one or two even finding their way
into the black plastic bags full of dog shit which dog owners
are so fond of displaying on fence posts and raggedy buddleia
skirting the edges of waste ground and are bursting forth.

These bean stalks potentially are springing up with the vigour
of something neglected in the cool, dry dark for too long,
waving ambitious tendrils above chimney pots and telegraph poles,
straining, straining to hear the far off song of a golden harp.

Niche

Niches fill with what you wish them to contain.
The recess in the temple's mosaic-laden wall
is thought to be filled with what is numinous.

The lamp burns in the darkness there,
in the silent penumbra lies the meeting of two worlds,
from such a retreat so much can be seen when one looks.

There is a simple niche in the crook of a summer oak's bough.
From there the infinite can be found in the layering of leaves,
from there even the tick of the sundial can be heard.

In this house though the numinous lives in the fireplace niche,
on the bookshelves, rattling the cutlery in the drawer, the spoons
and forks strain to accommodate all that is wished for them to hold.

Ash Wednesday

My Aunt breastfed my cousin when I was young
which was a good thing of course, although my mother
said that she'd 'never seemed the type', something to do
with thick pan make-up and chips, a connection
I didn't understand at the time. There were a lot of cousins
so the breastfeeding memory, though clear,
is most likely an amalgamation of many scenes,
and many babies, and many long afternoons in stuffy rooms.
However, it must have been coming up to Lent one year
on a visit that shows itself in particular relief,
when I sat watching her feed, watching the cigarette
as it burned in her mouth, waiting for the greying ashes
to drop on the newborn's brow, wondering if it would leave
a blurred mark to identify them
which would tell them where they belonged.

Blue Barrel

The blue barrel sits slumped, leaning
at a slackened angle into the laurel hedge
topless and stained, its moulded plastic
in sharp contrast to the mesh of daisy
and dandelion pushing up around its base —
a lurching drunk supported by vegetation.

It came from the other half of my semi,
kindly donated when I requested
by the developer's builder; well, more a labourer;
he appeared unskilled, always given the donkey work.
The lugging, the hacking, the shifting and shunting
and in confabs remained unconsulted.

The contents barely sloshed over when hoisted
by the diggerish machinery he drove.
They had already dug up a tremendous
patch of rhubarb and dismantled and disposed of
the garden shed which had twenty years of
Woodwork Magazine packed neatly inside.

I had been out that day.
But I was in time to get the blue barrel
filled with an elderly compost, thick crust on top
and when broken through, a rancid liquid festering beneath
that had once been grass cuttings
from a lawn that had once been mown.

Fabulous stuff, even though
the kids ran from the smell, shrieking,
then darting back again to confirm the stench.
And several years on the blue barrel still sits —
a strange memorial to have
to Jack who had lived next door.

Thirst

In the erotic art of feudal Japan
the protagonists are never shown kissing.
Within the intimate billows and folds
of material and limbs, the eyes are fixed
on the other's, but the lips are not.
I hold on to this knowledge when you drink
from my water bottle, then having returned it,
walk on. I hold the bottle with both hands
and drink deeply from what remains.

Best Years

I spent my twenties breastfeeding, pram pushing
and desperately filling in time in cafés and charity shops.
I knew each pensioner to greet and their dogs,
toured church halls, memorising on which morning
their doors would be open to the buggies helmed
by baggy-eyed mothers for whom a scone
and instant coffee could be manna.

I spent my twenties rising at 5.30 a.m. after endlessly
broken nights, somnolence fractured, summoned
by the mewling to pace humming softly, rocking,
bouncing, finding new ways to vibrate soothingly
and avoiding eye contact as though grizzling in my arms
I held a squirming Medusa, sleep-refusing, milky-breathed.

I spent my twenties going early to bed after watching
repeats on Dave of the cleverer comedy commentary shows
as the current series remained over my head,
having not watched the News for long swathes of time
as each attempt I made to view I would be reduced to tears.
weeping on the sticky sofa at my own helplessness.

I spent my twenties with pockets bulging filled with tissues,
shells and stones, the residue from sweetie wrappers
dulling only slightly the pearlescent sheen that had caught
a small child's eye as they stopped, suddenly halted
in a determined dash to a destination as yet undetermined;
a magpie glance, greedy, appraising, and claiming every treasure.

I spent my twenties shoving swings, watching roundabouts
go round and round, marvelling at the kinetic energy,
untapped sparkling and bursting out, shimmering like a haze
over the surface of Health and Safety-approved flooring
and new-fangled locks on chains thwarting attempts
to reach the height where it all goes slack.

In Iran the Fruit Trees are Everywhere

Trees sleep within their circadian cycle,
their cells deplete of water and the branches,
which had been embracing the light, untense
and with a supple ease rest through the night.

In B&Q the saplings are lit by fluorescent strip,
where a man and his son carry forth a Cherry Blossom
to the till to ask when it will bear fruit?
'In my country the fruit trees are everywhere.'

Heads are shaken sadly at the sterile blooms in his hands.
'Then you are lucky,' he is told.
'No, I am not lucky, not so lucky.'
Between them the young tree is returned to the rack.

Ladybird

Ladybirds when they fly reveal their hidden wings
of fine transparency, filigree-netted underthings
beneath the flouncing polka-dotted shell.
It is a game to count the spots, cupping hands around
in the hope she will not leave as she is so beautiful
but it is always when she wants to go
that the red skirt is raised and what is secret
delicately lifts her, swiftly taking her away.

Lower Spine

There is a place in the line of my lower back
curving down the taper of coccyx to vanished tail
where I imagine the knee of an elephant would mould;
the toe of its front right leg delicately pointed,
creating its own arch, my spine immaculately bowed
across the dome of that joint.

I would stretch back along the length of its thigh
sensing the full weight of the beast
redirected and dispersed over three legs only,
the tremble of position maintained
as my arms reach up, disappearing my hands
into the folds of its neck.

I can sense the invertebrate sway of the trunk,
exhaling warm hay-breath about my ankles,
the dry heat of its hide on my skin;
when I step away and it rests its foot
once more on the ground I smile —
for I'll know I will not be forgotten.

Patagonia

I have read there is a tribe living in the mountains
and lakes of Patagonia who can barely count beyond five,
yet have a language so precise there is a word for;
the curious experience of unexpectedly discovering
something spherical and precious in your mouth,
formed perhaps by grit finding its way into the shellfish
(such as an oyster) you have just eaten.
Or something like that. I identify with this conceptual position.
And as I listen to my children debate on the train
as to which is the greater — googolplex or infinity —
whilst knowing they still struggle with their 4 times table,
I can't help but reflect that maybe we should be
on a small canoe at great altitude, trailing
our semantic home spun nets behind instead.

Shop Steward Road Trip

The coach-filled fug of men and smoke can be savoured,
and perhaps pocketed for later, after the journey's end —
atmosphere made solid, ether so rich and full —
density taken from human conviction and given form —
bus shaped — fermenting from London to Stranraer
then preserved in brine on the ferry to Belfast.
They had marched, jeered at Callaghan's Caribbean tan,
bloated in indignation, ripe for the justice owed to them
(*but told my father to keep to the back as he was a Taig*).
On their return they took a democratic vote
to release some of the collected miasma and travel
via Stratford to visit Anne Hathaway's wee cottage,
stretch out their legs weary from Parliament Square,
have a bun, and send a postcard home.

Earwig

The linen trousers need pressing
before suitability for public appearance
and the iron is set, softly clicking
the tick of the element heating metal.

As the first leg is spread and misted
an anomaly in the translucent Perspex
of the iron's body catches the eye.
An earwig, panicked, struggling within.

It had gone to great lengths to be trapped
deciding in that whole room's vast expanse
the 1cm diameter of the water funnel
was the place it had to explore,

and now finds itself desperately paddling
in the water warming from tempered plate.
I watch, unable to help, and reason that drowning
in calescent water is no different to drowning in cold.

My ironing continues, smoothing the creases
front and back, pausing to observe the earwig's progress
now and again, refusing to feel responsibility
for its indignation at its own wilful demise.

Calligraphy

There is a copperplate swirl of buzzard
on wing above the wheat field
assessing the Morse-coded dash of wary rabbit
in its sporadic, foraging path.
Such elaborate curve of flight is perfectly controlled
by stroke of fingered-feathers on outermost reach
before making a calculated plunge to the quarry below.
My own dynamic of calligraphic flight
can more recognisably be seen
through the erratic bounce and dip
of swallow in its increasing anticipation of departure —
small inversions and sudden peaks, brief moments
of gliding bliss, these reflect the hand
which articulates each spiral bound page —
the widening gaps between words,
my right-tilted slant, unclosed loops
with generous curled tails and top-heavy strokes
means (as any Graphologist would know),
I am of my imagination but unreliable in affairs of the heart.
To read my life through the patterns I write,
through my drops and my twirls,
is to know I look South and desire,
like the swallow, to be gone.

You are My Selfish Thing

I witness the first flake of snow
before the blizzard falls.
The blizzard belongs to me.

The Three Graeae

Empyreal air is unfilled, voided
of gravity where Perseus should fall.
His lack travels mountainous cleft,
enters the cavity of shadow-marled cave,
finding copsed — the three Graeae.

Perseus abstracts from the sockets,
dislocates the glenoid of orbit and gum —
he takes what he needs and withdraws.
The succession of vacant space recedes,
absence and its opposite fades in the dusk.

Suds

It seems the floor was unclean
because as she scrubbed with the mop
the grey-edged suds grew from the polished wood
spreading from what had been dry
beneath the damp braids, and frothed
across the corridor, swelling against
the skirting boards and seeping
under door frames which remained
closed to her efforts.
Within those rooms the occupants
must have been alarmed by the rising tide —
what seemed like the scum from a restless sea
seeking them out to trace contour lines
with the drying of brine and debris
about their feet and desks.
Once at a park in the rain her small boy's head
began to foam, his hair smeared with secret,
unrinsed shampoo. Those bubbles rose
a little way, as far as they could dodge
the raindrops which had summoned them;
the iridescence dispersed before their raised eyes
with sudden pops.

Room

There was a room kept aside for the ghosts
in that large and well-appointed house,
a room that if windows were flung open
could summon up the Autumn winds,
call the gusts and crumbling leaves even if time
were only turning towards Llamas.
The room held an endless cool
close to itself — not dampness,
but a lingering on the walls,
a suggestion of something wreathed there
that dulled the ticking of the clock
and blurred the etchings, framed and hung.
The rest of the house welcomed the sun
like sand on a wooden floor
spilled and tipped with shaken blanket
and sandals from beach-trip return.
But footstep, unmeasured on stairs
would slow and quiet on passing the door
listening and hoping not to hear
those voices packed so carefully away
in the room kept aside for the ghosts.

Nietzsche vs. Childhood

'If we both lay down flat
we'd be the same height,'
said the child expansively.
His facial expression must have been
confused and wondering enough
not to need to speak the question
before it was answered —
'Well, if our feet were at
the same spot, then I'd be
almost to your shoulder.'
'Doesn't my head count?'
he asked. 'Not really,' she said.
Funny — he'd always thought that that
was the most important part.

Hamilton Graving Dock

In Belfast the sleech was hauled
from the banks of the Lagan,
grey sodden heaps of post mortem flesh,
flaccid with the weight of itself.
Water seeped through every pore
of that sand and mud
as fast as it could be pumped away
by wheezing engines spewing steam and fire,
and dredgers which yawned their metal jaws
to scoop, heave and retch the marled muck
whilst around the terraced graving dock
450 men erected their Lilliputian struts
about the vast form of some vanished, vacant beast.

Home

At home I step across the threshold,
across the sandbags filled with sodden bibles,
there to reassure the children who'd been told
without them the foundations of our abode
are unfixed and will wash away,
so I collected testaments old and new,
and filled the burlap bags for them.
They decorate the sacks with daisy chains
and special stones, step across the borders easily.
Inside we eat our ungraced meal
and then climb into unknelt-by beds.

Celestial Mechanics

In the midst of things did it seem ordinary,
the movement of one moment to the next
a series of 'and then... and then... and then...'
that seemed normal when you were engrossed?
Or was there a point in Space
when you looked from the Vostok
and saw the world was blue,
saw the absence of God,
and you marvelled at the path,
from the making of moulds
to the mechanics of the celestial,
as you made orbit of your home?
Perhaps the accumulation of your time
only made its fantastical arc apparent
in the unexpected moments left to you
between the rush of sonic boom and
your sudden, endless tail-spin,
a Mobius fall to Earth.

One Day

So much can happen in one day.
The Sphinx knew it and built a reputation upon it,
metaphor folded tight in his constructed origami play,
until Oedipus pulled hard, tugged with an expert reply
which scythed through the seams, sprung the trap
and severed the Sphinx from his life.
Yes, much can occur in a single day.
In a single day the Sun is born, leaves his mother's arms,
fills the sky before facing the fact of his descent
to be nursed in old age once more at her breast.
In Slavic lore the agéd child needs held through the night —
when the glowing ember of the heart needs care
whilst the Moon Chasers shriek about their heads,
she tends his failing light in the dark, until pulling free
he climbs the blue anew. She waits below the horizon,
anticipates his return. Much can happen in one day.

Seaweed

The seaweed dries slowly, small decorative curls
which have been artfully spread amongst the stone
and shell scavenged from the beach.

As the seaweed dries salt crystallises on the rubbery skin
and as it dries farther and the moisture evaporates entirely
the tiny crystals drop and lie without direction on the sill.

Inspection shows how precisely formed they are —
cubic solids on a minute scale. Midst careful arrangement
of conch and pebble this fallen saline is perfection.

The Burden of Stone

The Egyptian Goddess Nut sprawls across the heavens,
or apparently she is the heavens, holding down form and order
and keeping the chaos out, although it's hard to know
which way she prefers to face.
In Greece it is Hera who decorates that expanse;
her milk in fountain spray from suddenly unbabied breast
splatters the Milky Way before composure is recovered.
Both are heifers really, tender, swollen udders hanging low
and their difficulties lie, not in the weight which pushes in
from above, but in the hot ache of flesh stretched thin,
finding the right vessel to fill, rivers to flood, heroes to nurse.
They have no time for the quiet burden of gravity
causing shoulders and necks to seize in unnatural curves,
which is a millstone on the brow — the burden of stone
bearing down on the Earth, unable to look up at the sky.

Rumpelstiltskin

I felt dizzy as though I could step into the lights
I told her my depth perception was gone

but she had taken the thick glasses from her eyes
and lost herself in bright smears and streaks

so I continued to be confused by the fireworks and stars
and the distant headlamps on far lough shore.

She said something should emerge from the swirls in the air
called by the ignited runes that illuminate the dark.

But we've come every year to watch and wait
wrapped tight against the wind and the rain

and every year we've turned and walked home
still without having named the unknown.

Hen Sitting

The hens vocalise incessantly.
Small querulous gulps,
as the ark is circled by magpies,
puzzled by the loss of
their usual right to scraps.
They're carefully ignored,
industrious scrabbling in dirt
more rewarding than
petty piebald stares.
It is not innocence though,
this bucolic infestation,
Xhosa clicks passed among themselves,
the little warblings and pops,
depth charges tracking my passage —
I am observed and feel uneasy.
In obsidian eye
too much Raptor remains.

Beyond the Mussel Banks

On the Lough's shore it is possible to find partially knapped flints,
rejected as arrow heads when the line of fracture
was not right — a misjudged strike by the knapping stone.
The chippings have been ground to sand by the tides,
lost as varying shades of grit compress in the damp,
unnoticed when trailing across the beach by the tideline —
picking a path carefully in May to avoid the ragworms'
death throes above their hidden eggs, and in August
when the lea shimmers with dissolving corpses of jellyfish.
There is no liberty found here mixed with splinters of shells
and rotting sea brack, the soft parts of dying things
and the broken fragments of what was intended to fly —
but beyond the mussel banks I have ridden the wake
of the ferries, astride the prow of the fishing boats
shoulders untensed and neck unbowed in the lash of the brine
where, from the dissipating crest of each wave, my cry was barbaric.

The Rivets

The rivets are frozen overnight.
It must be some engineer's job
at the end of the day
to drop the shaped alloy
into the liquid nitrogen cauldron
before heading home for supper,
tongs laid carefully on the bench
with the thick protective rubber gloves beside
ready for the morning.
In the aircraft assembly building
the component parts are waiting;
on the wing the holes are drilled
matching the bores on the fuselage.
With the early shift the men must be swift,
the contraction of steel with freezing
only gives a spare millimetre
and the thaw happens fast.
It must be impressive to watch;
the hoisting of wing to body,
vapour rising from the frozen vats,
the choreography of rivets lifted, fitted,
blunt end hammered to the plate
as it is slotted into place,
the expansion of the bolt fixing it all —
the wing to the plane, the plane to the sky,
the beautiful genius of that rapid dance
carried out to the ringing of metal
in the vastness of that vaulted space.

Everything was Tidied Away

Everything was tidied away.
She'd started with the clothes on the line
when, standing at the kitchen window,
she saw how it all was in disarray.
So the washing was rehung, ordered
according to colour and size, graduating
the length of the rope, with coordinating pegs.
What did not fit was discretely hidden away.
The children had been bothering her
but she found it helped when she had them stand still
from tallest to smallest, although there was consternation
when it was noticed that this did not go evenly
from eldest to youngest due to a particularly gangly six-year-old
however, when the importance of order was explained to him
he willingly bent his knees to keep the peace.
The garden was next, all those untidy bushes
and masses of dreaming petals were split
into their component parts, laid neatly on the lawn,
the finer leaves fixed to their spot with the aid
of some superglue in case of the event
of any unplanned breezes to upset the precise drills.
By this time it was edging to night.
She rose up onto the points of her toes
to pluck each star as it appeared to be strung
evenly as a string of beads, wrapped in regular coils,
the vague spatter of Milky Way now presented
as a satisfying thread of lights in banal display
It was with relief then that she could finally rest,
to sleep deep on the crisp starched sheets of her bed.

Bullfinch

I had almost forgotten you'd given me chocolate
that I'd stored in my bedside drawer to keep safe,
but, when recalled, the anticipation of the small gift
waiting in the wooden dark within my room, amongst fronds
of desiccated lavender, was enough to raise the hairs of nape.
From the window I watch a bullfinch, its plumage
a small sunset midst early buds of plum tree by the wall,
methodically stripping each potential fruit from axil scale
until the tree stands topless, girdled only by a low hem of blooms.
I unwrap the chocolate and hear the finch's melancholy call.

Brick

The warmth of the brick wall
comes as a shock after so much time spent
hunched into the Nor-Easterly.
My red swing coat buffeted and splayed,
flapping against the sudden tugs,
an excess of material that came at such expense
no match for a wind
that has travelled here from Siberia
and will continue across this land
gathering up the baby birds and coconut scent of gorse
until finding the Atlantic.
No, my coat is no match for that.
But somewhere, beyond the scudding clouds
the sun has insinuated with steady pulse
an unnoticed heat, infiltrating the inanimate
like the fable I used to love.
And even though I may not feel inclined
to loosen any buttons,
I press my back to the wall
and take my comfort there.

Only Imaginary Things

Only imaginary things are fought for
wealth
borders
religion.
I fight you for my heart;
I can see it there
trembling in your hand.

Mad Red

after 'The Potato Diggers' by Paul Henry

I am Mad Red in the bog
with the boots you lent to me
three sizes too big and squelching.

I watch where the bog water collects
and dream of crashing cataracts
and I hear them too, far off,
though not seen in this moss stew
I'm currently standing in.

Your rain coat is tied about my hips
low slung from the weight of the pockets
filled with white and yellow quartz

and I climb to find the biggest expanse
with a sense of timelessness and placelessness
and magic to etch itself on to me,
startling the sheep by my stumble.

I think I can pick the thin reed of smoke
from our cottage cutting its heated way
through the mists and I want to find the thing
that will take me out of myself
but instead realise I have always been Mad Red.

Wren

The wren moves with a zeotropic grace;
sudden jumps and skips causing it to appear
and disappear in unexpected places —
a magical illusion of secret clockwork powers.
It rises suddenly, vanishing into the nano-fineness
of the ice-edged morning air.

The Island

It's an odd journey, a priest going one way, a pony the other,
although both with eyes fastened on the island's shore,
as desperation likes a lump of rock in the sea to hold on to,
the rock of the island standing firm against all the sea can muster.
The farewell party on the beach have returned their flat caps
to their respectful heads, awaiting the horse's arrival on a curragh
currently straining against the tide, slowing that approach
as much as it speeds the Father to the mainland.
There're four men working each boat, each pulling on the oars
whilst poised at the prow (high risen to pierce every wave
regardless its strength) are the transported; neither horse
nor priest glance to the side when their paths cross,
one gaze fixed forward, the other to the diminishing rear,
each anticipating the work still needing to be done.

Observations

Some things deserve their privacy.
When the rustle in the hedgerow
does not require examination,
the twisted vines and tangled growth
hold those beating hearts that must learn
to still, learn not to startle
at any stranger's unbidden approach;
that in the silent groves
and bark-wrought kingdoms
those little lives run without any keeping
watch from aside. I know the sense
of the hollow bones and virgin feathers
cupped in my hand, the muted drumroll
of the heart — but it is not my task
to reach into those greening thickets
and pluck them out once more.

Pruning

'Scottish pruning' my sister named it
as we watched my father from the kitchen window
methodically chomping with the shears
at the rapidly diminishing lilac.
Such managerial directness applied to
such unnecessary maintenance.
My father, oblivious to his being observed,
his shirt neatly tucked into belted trousers,
top button fastened and tie fastidiously knotted,
carefully depleted the abundance
the untamed and the wild.
'Everything looks stunted,' I complained.
'Nothing touches.'
'Your father doesn't like the mess from the blossom,'
replied my mother, bustling by with a duster in hand.
My sister and I turned back to the window.

Totem

In the museum was a pine trunk, 8,600 years old, standing
totem-tall, un-anthropomorphised, signifier only of itself.
Nearby smaller sections — oak (4,000 years) and yew (5,000 years) —
had been dug from the bog, placed on a plinth, brought,
startled, into the light, from their soft dark sleep in the peat.

I stretched out to touch what had been wrought in darkness,
rubbed my finger tips across the distortions of the piece —
texture like butter from the fridge — realised the polish I felt
had been given by other furtive devotions by other visitors
on the forbidden wood, feeling what otherwise wouldn't be known.

Later that evening, after several single malts,
you lifted the antique woodblock mould of the acanthus
down from its display in the rented cottage.
We kneaded the grain with olive oil from the kitchen
then pressed the cheap clay we'd bought into its writhing form.

Days after the clay had dried and you'd your cast to bring home
I continued to slip my fingers into the inverse creviced curves,
gazing from my windowed desk at the mountain's southern flank
where shades of clouds continually passed and where, below,
the sun glinted intermittently on the black waters of the Lough.

ACKNOWLEDGEMENTS

Acknowledgements are due to the following publications in which versions of some of these poems first appeared: *Project 365+1*, *The Honest Ulsterman*, *Abridged*, *The Galway Review*, *FourXFour*, *Urban Myths and Legends* (The Emma Press), *The Incubator*, *The Linnet's Wing*, *Compass Magazine*, *Writing Motherhood* (Seren Press), *Skylight 47*, *Shift Lit*, *Animals Anthology* (The Emma Press), *Panning for Poems*, *Wild Atlantic Words*, *Matter* (LaVa), *Connections* (LaVa) and *Reflexion*.

Many thanks are due to Lisa and John at Doire Press, the ACNI (especially Damian Smyth), to the many editors who published my work, to Poetry NI, and to Liz Dunn and Maire Logue from Listowel Writers' Week. I also wish to thank Fionn and Bram for being the hallions that they are, and most of all, Philip for his endless patience, honest critiques and love.

EMMA MCKERVEY won the 2015 PoetryNI / Translink Poetry Competition and in 2016 she was shortlisted for both the NI National Poetry Competition and the Bord Gáis Irish Book Awards' Poem of the Year Award. In 2017 she had two poems highly commended for the Seamus Heaney Prize. She is also a professionally-trained musician, having played cello in orchestras, saxophone in various jazz ensembles and developed sonic art performance pieces with a range of composers, collaborating with dancers and theatre practitioners on both islands. A member of Women Aloud, Emma is from Holywood, County Down. *The Rag Tree Speaks* is her debut collection.